Dear Parent:
Your child's love of reading starts here!

Every child learns to read in a different way and at his or her own speed. Some go back and forth between reading levels and read favorite books again and again. Others read through each level in order. You can help your young reader improve and become more confident by encouraging his or her own interests and abilities. From books your child reads with you to the first books he or she reads alone, there are I Can Read Books for every stage of reading:

SHARED READING
Basic language, word repetition, and whimsical illustrations, ideal for sharing with your emergent reader

BEGINNING READING
Short sentences, familiar words, and simple concepts for children eager to read on their own

READING WITH HELP
Engaging stories, longer sentences, and language play for developing readers

READING ALONE
Complex plots, challenging vocabulary, and high-interest topics for the independent reader

ADVANCED READING
Short paragraphs, chapters, and exciting themes for the perfect bridge to chapter books

I Can Read Books have introduced children to the joy of reading since 1957. Featuring award-winning authors and illustrators and a fabulous cast of beloved characters, I Can Read Books set the standard for beginning readers.

A lifetime of discovery begins with the magical words "I Can Read!"

Visit www.icanread.com for information
on enriching your child's reading experience.

*I dedicate this book to the
modern freedom fighters
who refuse to be silent.
—N.L.H.*

*I dedicate this book to the
Adelante Africa and
El Pájaro Azúl Foundations.
—G.M.*

Special thanks to Dr. Kate Larson, author and historian, for her valuable assistance.

Author's note: There are few records documenting Tubman's life. Since Tubman herself couldn't read or write, all the stories about her have been told by others. After the Civil War, Sarah Bradford wrote two books about Harriet Tubman. The books contained interviews with Tubman, but they also contained mistakes and details that historians now believe were exaggerated (like how many rescue missions she made). And not much was written about Tubman's Civil War years. Researchers have since gathered more information using oral histories and letters.

Picture credits:
Page 29: The Wanted Notice is reproduced courtesy of Jay and Susan Meredith, Bucktown Village Foundation. The photo of Harriet Tubman at age forty-six is by Benjamin F. Powelson and is used courtesy of the Library of Congress and the National Museum of African American History and Culture.
Page 30: Map image used under license from Shutterstock.com.
The following images are © Getty Images: Tubman on page 28, engraving of Tubman circa 1865 by Hulton Archive and Tubman and her family by George Eastman Museum on page 31, the Home for the Aged by Epics on page 32.

Harriet Tubman: Freedom Fighter
Copyright © 2019 by HarperCollins Publishers
All rights reserved. Manufactured in U.S.A.
No part of this book may be used or reproduced in any manner whatsoever without written permission except in the case of brief quotations embodied in critical articles and reviews. For information address HarperCollins Children's Books, a division of HarperCollins Publishers, 195 Broadway, New York, NY 10007.
www.icanread.com

Library of Congress Control Number: 2018946036
ISBN 978-0-06-243285-8 (trade bdg.)— ISBN 978-0-06-243284-1 (pbk.)

Book design by Rick Farley

20 21 22 LSCC 10 9 8 7

❖ First Edition

I Can Read!

READING 2 WITH HELP

HARRIET TUBMAN

Freedom Fighter

by Nadia L. Hohn
pictures by Gustavo Mazali

HARPER

An Imprint of HarperCollinsPublishers

Harriet Tubman was no ordinary hero.

As a woman and a slave,

she had no rights and was not taught

how to read or write.

She also had a disability.

None of that stopped her from

leading many people to freedom.

Harriet Tubman was born enslaved
in 1822 in Maryland.
Everyone in her family was enslaved.
As a slave, Harriet could be sold
like an animal or a house
by a white slave master.

Slaves had to work for no pay.
Many slaves lived and worked
on small farms and plantations.
They were treated badly.

We know her as Harriet Tubman,
but when she was born
her name was Araminta "Minty" Ross.
When Minty was a girl in the 1800s
slavery was no longer allowed
in the northern states in America,
but Maryland was a southern state.

When Minty was three,

her sister Mariah Ritty was sold.

And soon after that,

Minty's sister Linah was sold, too.

They were taken away from the family.

Soon after, Minty was loaned out
to work at other plantations.
Once she had to rock a baby
all night so it wouldn't cry.
If the baby cried, Minty was whipped.

Another time Minty had to take
muskrats out of a trap
while wading in an icy marsh,
even though she was sick.
Minty knew that slavery was wrong.
As she grew older, she started
to think about escape.

One day Minty went to the store.

A slave master threw a heavy weight

at a slave who was trying to flee.

Instead, Minty was hit on the head.

She fainted and bled a lot.

Minty woke up weeks later.

But this injury caused a disability.

Minty had seizures and headaches
for the rest of her life.

Minty started having vivid dreams
in which God gave her guidance.

When Minty was a young adult,

her slave master died.

The slaves on his farm knew

that they might be sold far away.

For Minty, this meant that

her family that she loved so much

might be separated

and never see each other again.

Harriet Tubman,

as she then called herself,

and two of her brothers

tried to escape but turned back

because the punishment would

be huge.

Harriet decided to escape again.

Alone and with no map,

she prayed that God would lead her.

Harriet traveled north

through the Underground Railroad.

The Underground Railroad

didn't have trains.

It was a group of people,

both black and white,

who helped freedom seekers escape.

Sometimes the help

was a safe place to hide.

Hiding places were called stations.

The helpers were called conductors.

When Harriet got to Philadelphia,

Pennsylvania, she was free.

For months she worked in the city.

She missed her family,

who were still enslaved.

So she saved all her money

and used it to go back south

to help free her family.

The trip south was dangerous.

If found by slavecatchers,

slaves were returned to slavery,

hurt, or killed.

Despite the enormous danger,

Harriet kept going back.

When the Fugitive Slave Act
was passed in 1850,
Philadelphia became too unsafe
for Harriet and her family.
So they went all the way to
St. Catharines, in Canada, to live.

But Harriet still returned
to the United States to free
more slaves.
She moved by foot, boat, train,
and wagon.
She often wore disguises.
She was never caught.

In 1861, the Civil War began between the North and the South. The North formed the Union Army and the South formed the Confederate Army.

The Union Army fought
to keep the United States
from breaking apart.

Wanting to help end slavery,
Harriet signed up black men
to be soldiers in the Union Army.
She worked as a cook, a nurse,
and a spy.

Harriet freed slaves
as the army moved.
She even led a battle.

When the war ended in 1865,

slavery ended.

Harriet believed in freedom for all

until the day she died.

She said,

"I should fight for my liberty

so long as my strength lasted."

Timeline

1822

Araminta "Minty" Ross is born in Dorchester County, Maryland.

1844

Minty Ross changes her name to Harriet Tubman.

1849

Harriet escapes from enslavement.

1850–1860

Tubman leads about thirteen escapes through the Underground Railroad to Philadelphia and Canada.

1861

The Civil War begins and Tubman works as a nurse, a cook, and a spy for the Union Army.

1865

The Civil War ends, and slavery ends, too.

1869

Tubman marries Nelson Davis.

1913

Tubman dies in Auburn, New York.

1830
1840
1850
1860
1870
1880
1890
1900
1910

Was Tubman old when she made her amazing escape and rescues?

No! All the photographs of Harriet Tubman were taken after the end of the Civil War. She was in her twenties when she started helping enslaved people escape.

Hoarriet Tubman

This is the earliest known photo of Tubman. She was about forty-six.

THREE HUNDRED DOLLARS REWARD.

RANAWAY from the subscriber on Monday the 17th ult., three negroes, named as follows: HARRY, aged about 19 years, has on one side of his neck a wen, just under the ear, he is of a dark chestnut color, about 5 feet 8 or 9 inches hight; BEN, aged about 25 years, is very quick to speak when spoken to, he is of a chestnut color, about six feet high; MINTY, aged about 27 years, is of a chestnut color, fine looking, and about 5 feet high. One hundred dollars reward will be given for each of the above named negroes, if taken out of the State, and $50 each if taken in the State. They must be lodged in Baltimore, Easton or Cambridge Jail, in Maryland.

ELIZA ANN BRODESS,
Near Bucktown, Dorchester county, Md.
Oct. 3d, 1849.

☞The Delaware Gazette will please copy the above three weeks, and charge this office.

Wanted notice for Harriet Tubman

Slavery was illegal in Pennsylvania. Why did Tubman start taking enslaved people all the way to Canada?

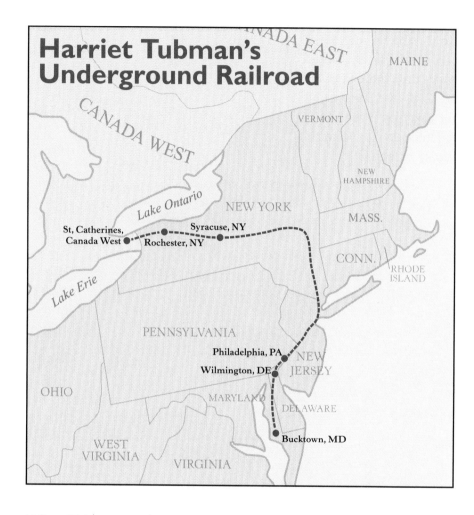

Harriet Tubman's Underground Railroad

CANADA EAST

MAINE

CANADA WEST

VERMONT

NEW HAMPSHIRE

Lake Ontario

NEW YORK

MASS.

St, Catherines, Canada West

Rochester, NY

Syracuse, NY

CONN.

RHODE ISLAND

Lake Erie

PENNSYLVANIA

Philadelphia, PA

NEW JERSEY

Wilmington, DE

OHIO

MARYLAND

DELAWARE

WEST VIRGINIA

VIRGINIA

Bucktown, MD

When Tubman was born in Maryland, slavery was not legal in the northern United States. Slavery was outlawed in Canada in 1834, when Tubman was twelve. At first, Tubman guided escaping enslaved people to the northern state of Pennsylvania, which bordered Maryland. But in 1850, the US government passed the Fugitive Slave Act, which said that escaped slaves must be returned to slavery if they were caught in a northern state. Staying in Philadelphia, Pennsylvania, was no longer safe, and Harriet Tubman started guiding escaping freedom seekers all the way to St. Catharines, Ontario, in Canada.

How many people did Tubman rescue?

Tubman rescued around seventy people over thirteen trips to Maryland. Harriet Tubman also played an important and pioneering role in the Civil War. At the request of the Union Army, Tubman enlisted black soldiers to fight and also organized black men to spy for the army, while working as a spy herself. Her spying gave important information to Union officers about where Confederate soldiers were stationed. In 1863, Tubman led troops in a raid that destroyed Southern bridges and railroad lines. That mission freed 750 slaves—men, women, and children. Tubman was the first woman in US history to lead a military battle.

What did Tubman do after the Civil War?

Harriet Tubman married Nelson Davis, a former soldier. The couple adopted a daughter and fostered other children. Family remained incredibly important to Tubman, and in Auburn, New York, she was reunited with her parents and other relatives. Tubman continued an active life of public service, making speeches to help women get the vote and establishing an old age home for African Americans.

Harriet is on the left, next to her is her adopted daughter, Gertie Davis, and her husband, Nelson Davis.

Places to Visit

Harriet Tubman National Historical Park
Auburn, NY
Visitors can go to the Harriet Tubman Visitor Center, the Tubman Home for the Aged, and the Harriet Tubman Residence, as well as the Thompson Memorial African Methodist Episcopal Zion Church that Tubman raised funds to build.
https://www.nps.gov/hart/index.htm

Home for the Aged in Auburn, NY

Harriet Tubman Underground Railroad State Park and National Historical Park
Church Creek, MD
Visit the Harriet Tubman Underground Railroad Visitor Center, which is the gateway to the **Harriet Tubman Underground Railroad Scenic Byway**. The byway is a 125-mile drive along Maryland's Eastern Shore that includes thirty-six places tied to the Underground Railroad.
https://www.nps.gov/hatu/index.htm
http://dnr.maryland.gov/publiclands/pages/eastern/tubman.aspx
http://harriettubmanbyway.org

National Museum of African American History and Culture
Washington, DC
https://nmaahc.si.edu